Miami Beach

David Scheinbaum

Foreword by Beaumont Newhall

Essay by Stephen M. Fain

Miami Beach

Photographs of an American Dream

Florida International University Press / Miami

Published in the U.S.A. on acid-free paper.

Library of Congress Cataloging-in-Publication Data

Scheinbaum, David, 1951–
    Miami Beach: photographs of an American dream / David
    Scheinbaum; foreword by Beaumont Newhall; essay by
    Stephen M. Fain.
    p.   cm.
    ISBN 0-8130-0933-2 (cloth). — ISBN 0-8130-1031-4 (paper)
    1. Miami (Fla.)—Description—Views.   2. Aged—
    Florida—Miami—Pictorial works.   3. Aged—Florida—
    Miami.   4. Miami (Fla.)—Social conditions—Pictorial
    works.   I. Fain, Stephen M., 1940.   II. Title.
    F319.M6S34   1990
    975.9'381—dc20   90-3649

The Florida International University Press is a member of
University Presses of Florida, the scholarly publishing agency
of the State University System of Florida. Books are selected
for publication by faculty editorial committees at each of
Florida's nine public universities: Florida A&M University
(Tallahassee), Florida Atlantic University (Boca Raton), Florida
International University (Miami), Florida State University
(Tallahassee), University of Central Florida (Orlando), Univer-
sity of Florida (Gainesville), University of North Florida
(Jacksonville), University of South Florida (Tampa), Univer-
sity of West Florida (Pensacola).

Orders for books published by all member presses should be
addressed to University Presses of Florida, 15 NW 15th St.,
Gainesville, FL 32603.

To the memory of my grandfather, Hyman Fierman (Feerman)

My grandfather was born in an area known as Russia/Poland in 1894. He arrived in America aboard the *USS George Washington* in 1908. At age fourteen he had already been a butcher's apprentice, and he continued his apprenticeship in this country. One of his life's ambitions was fulfilled after his discharge from the U.S. Army on April 12, 1920: he became a citizen of the United States of America. He married in 1923 and opened his own butcher shop in Brooklyn, New York. In 1941, he gave up the shop, and for the remainder of his working years he was active as a butcher and a union member. At age sixty-five he retired.

Immediately after my grandmother's death on December 13, 1971, my grandfather resettled to Miami Beach, where he died in 1977. He is buried in Lodi, New Jersey, alongside my grandmother. His life and experiences inspired this project.

This work is dedicated to him.

Contents

Foreword

*T*o view the social scene with the camera is a challenge. All too often the photographer brings to his vision a priori judgments of what aspects of the people and their environment to record—so that we see with his mind rather than through his eyes. Or, if on assignment to a magazine, he may be forced to follow a shooting script or a briefing, so that he sees with the mind of an editor.

Conversely, the photographer may be prone to record those aspects of the scene that appeal to his pictorial sense—finding beautiful abstract compositions and novel subject matter which, though appealing, are but sidelights to the main issue.

It is yet more difficult to photograph a small, tight community bounded by two perimeters: ethnic ties and old age. To this challenge David Scheinbaum has responded with sympathy and understanding. He shows us what it is like to live in retirement in Miami Beach, Florida.

These photographs explain a situation little known to most of us. We are led along the sidewalks, into shops and gaming halls and the very homes of this community, by a compassionate yet observant and knowledgeable guide, seeing through his eyes.

Preface

Soon after my grandmother's death in 1971, my grandfather moved to Miami Beach. It did not take Grandpa long to shed the immigrant lifestyle that he had been living for sixty years. In one month's time he was wearing white slacks, white shoes, and wraparound sunglasses. Gone forever were the heavy dark overcoat and wool cap.

Those first years in Miami Beach were his happiest. The American Dream was now a reality. Grandpa took a long-awaited and hoped-for trip to Israel, which he couldn't do when Grandma was alive because she wouldn't fly. He even stopped questioning my long hair and jeans. Retirement was wonderful. Miami Beach was a land of sunshine, leisure, and safety: it was the land of milk and honey in America.

This is the dream of all of America's elderly: to be able to relax after a long life of hard work, and to have the time to come to terms with one's own life as it nears its end. For one large group of Americans, American Jews, Miami Beach has long been the place to fulfill this dream. Unfortunately, many of the retired elderly are in fact living impoverished and unhappy lives. The promised land exists for only a handful of people. The $500 monthly Social Security check does not get them through the month. Food, housing, and medical costs are all rising, while the check stays relatively the same. Some men and women live together to help each other financially, hiding the arrangement from their children out of embarrassment, unable to marry due to the partial loss of Social Security payments that would result. Many are unable to go to temple for lack of transportation and are unable to take advantage of the free lunch programs offered because the food is not strictly kosher.

I spoke with many people who had innumerable stories to share, stories of leaving the old country, struggling for work, organizing unions, and modifying their religious beliefs. These Jewish immigrants helped to build our America. As one elderly gentleman told me, "This is the last generation of its kind. What we have here is millions of years of experience walking around. Surely, millions of years of knowledge could still make a contribution to American life?"

When my grandfather's health began to fail he took to staying in his hotel room, forced to keep his swollen legs raised, often missing his daily pinochle game. I thought that his reclusiveness was the result of embarrassment. It was not. If the management of the hotel discovered that his health was failing, he would be asked to leave. So Grandpa, like many others, spent much of his time in his room, the prospect of a nursing home looming in his future.

When I arrived in Miami Beach, a stranger with a camera, I was welcomed everywhere I went. I was included in card and shuffleboard games and conversations. I was graciously invited into many homes. The company was wonderful, the conversations memorable and revealing, and for an introduction all I ever needed to do was answer yes to "Nuu . . . you're Jewish?"

These photographs record the visits into the lives that I was invited to share.

Acknowledgments

In a project like this, there are many people to thank. First, I would like to acknowledge all the people who permitted me to photograph them and invited me into their homes, and the many people who attended my exhibitions and presentations and helped me define and clarify the project as it progressed. They include Marvin Surkin, Max Serchuck, the Dade County Council of Senior Citizens, Al and Betty Block, Shirley Leone, Neil Trager, and Harvey Licht. Special thanks go to Beaumont Newhall for his help in editing the photographs for their first exhibition and for his foreword to the book; to Janet Russek, my wife, for her help with my text and captions and for the sequencing of the photographs for this book; to Deidre Bryan, my editor and liaison at the University Presses of Florida; and finally to Stephen Fain for his insightful essay.

Images of Miami Beach

I remember the coconut that hung in my friend's bedroom when I was a child. It was carved to look like a scowling face, but it was painted black, white, yellow, and red, with seashell earrings hanging on black leather straps; and it looked friendly. I was told it came from a tropical paradise where my friend's grandma lived and he sometimes visited. I knew where his grandma was because on a colorful blue ribbon were the words "Souvenir of Miami Beach" in gold. I remember thinking, *Someday I'll get there and I'll see the coconuts growing on the palm trees.*

Other images of Miami Beach came through other media: postcard pictures of beautiful, suntanned girls basking in the sun on sandy beaches, and hand-painted sailfish on the silk ties worn by those who had been there or had received the ties as gifts. Again I thought, *Someday I'll get there and I'll see the bathing beauties and walk on the warm, smooth sandy beach and catch my own sailfish.*

But most of all I remember what I heard the adults say about Miami Beach: "No snow and ice, it's nice all year around." "The summers are hotter than hell, with so much humidity." "It would be a good place for Mom and Pop. Lots of old folks really like it . . . the hotel is kosher and the room is clean . . . ocean air . . . what could be better . . . it's a perfect place for them. They can come home in the summer for a visit and we can take the train south for a visit in the winter."

"What do you mean they won't like it? There's a kosher butcher shop on every other corner and they've got a delicatessen and a *shul* on every block. . . . If an apartment costs too much they can go to the Shore Club or even the Ritz . . . look, it's Miami Beach, it's just right for them."

Every Jewish comedian seems to have a mother he is keeping in Miami

Beach. "It must be the perfect place because famous people tell you that they put their parents there in hotels and apartments." "Do you know anybody who would tell an audience that they put Mom and Pop in a home?" "The beach is a good place for them. They'll go and they'll love it."

"The little one thinks it paradise and the kids think it's for us. Who's to argue? What do we really have here? At least in Miami Beach we'll be with others like us. It's warm and there's no snow and ice. We'll make friends . . . it's a place to go and live."

From 17th Street to 96th Street

The sweeping lines of the Fontainebleau Hotel on Collins Avenue on the ocean and the ever-expanding Mount Sinai Hospital on the bay define the east-west width of the strip of land known as Miami Beach. The length of the beach runs from South Point to Surfside and beyond—all the way to opulent Bal Harbour and its once "restricted" enclave. If the soul of Miami Beach is in South Beach, then its heart is somewhere between Lincoln Road in the south and 96th Street in the north.

Leave South Beach and drive north on Collins Avenue—bear left before encountering the amazing *trompe l'oeil* mural on the wall of the Fontainebleau. Here begins the Miami Beach of Arthur Godfrey and Jackie Gleason. The Eden Roc with its kosher Chinese restaurant, the Fontainebleau with its upscale shops and ballrooms, its tropical-paradise pool and beach, and the Club Tropigala fuel the imaginations of tourists from around the world. Other impressive edifices loom over the winding avenue—the Alexander Hotel and the Sea Coast Towers condominiums, the Hirschfield Theater in the Clarion Castle, and the elegant Doral. Here the rich and the almost rich find comfort knowing that all of this is for them. The architecture is glitzy, and the buildings shield the beach and the ocean from the not so glitzy.

Collins Avenue is like the Colorado River meandering through the Grand Canyon. Instead of the rich earth tones of the sandstone walls of the natural canyon, "Collins Ave" moves north and south between walls of golden brick and stucco painted in tropical pinks, purples, blues, whites, and yellows. Traffic on Collins, the sidewalkers, and the activity on the beach signal the seasons, of which there really are only two: the season and not.

This is a place for manicures and pedicures, beauty and barber shops, and luxurious massages. This is where you'll find expensive elegance and cheap bargains for locals and international travelers. This is Miami Beach.

2

Across from the motorboat rentals on Indian Creek is yet another Miami Beach. The permanent residents live in island communities—some Jewish, some not. On LaGorce Drive there are Mediterranean villas and lots of old money—not very Jewish. But Miami Beach is a community—very Jewish.

Orthodox Jews often surround their community with a wire strung on poles as a way of marking what is inside and outside of the community; this is called an *erev*. If one were strung from Temple Beth Sholom (Reform) to the Hebrew Academy (Modern Orthodox) to Temple Emanu-El (Conservative) and back again, the Jewish community of Miami Beach would be unified and defined. Although the community looks whole to the outside, it is, in fact, very diversified within.

South Beach

From Joe's Stone Crab Restaurant in the south and north to the shops on Lincoln Road—from the causeway at Fifth Street to the Ocean Drive and the beach—here one finds South Beach, where many dreams retire to face *life after living*.

Life on South Beach is like life no place else! The smells of coconut oil and wintergreen blend and produce a fragrance that celebrates life and relieves stiff joints. On Miami Beach they worship Sol, but on South Beach they fear and respect Mount Sinai.

South Beach is Jewish, and much more. It is a collection of northern cities—New York, Boston, Detroit, Philadelphia, and Newark—dislocated and re-affirmed on a landscape of tropical beaches, disintegrating buildings poured out of weak and often rotting concrete, and a human spirit which affirms life while squarely facing pain, poverty, and the humiliation of dependency. Here meager pensions, Social Security, food stamps, and Jewish community services are blended together in a recipe for living by caring volunteers and professionals who work to ease the pain.

The choices really aren't many. One can stay at the Savoy Plaza on the beach or at the Astor or Kenmore Hotel on Washington Avenue. There are rooms of all types and sizes available, and the selection of a place to live is important. Your place is a good place if you can find a match between your income and the rent. Your place is a good place as long as you are healthy. If you lose your health, you can lose your place.

There are pullmanettes, kitchenettes, and efficiencies. There are food plans, dining rooms, food stamps, and restaurants (kosher and non-). Maids and room service are there for the buying; some places have pools and some people use them. Along the long sandy beaches and in the small shaded parks, South Beach is defined by the people and the footprints they leave in the sand every day.

Card Players

At "The Beach," life is what you make it. If you play cards you can join a group for pinochle, canasta, gin rummy, or casino. Some of the ladies play mah-jongg. For many these games provide links that connect strangers in chains of friendships and serve as conduits through which life histories are exchanged and sometimes created.

Some players seek the air-conditioned lobby of a small hotel where all the regulars have a place and an identity. Others choose the outdoors—by the pool, in the park, or on the beach—as the setting for the game. Although specific locations sometimes become territorial issues, in general there is order and peace.

The players are savvy. They know where to place a table to avoid a draft, and they know where the light is best when they play inside. They use string tied around the folding card table to form a grid, under which they securely place the cards so as to thwart the wind, the enemy of the outdoor card player. Table placement is, for many, just as important as the game—in fact, it is a part of the game. Inside or out, territoriality is an issue among the card players; once a spot is taken, it is taken. Those who play respect the territories of others and jealously guard their own. Those who watch the play understand this and always go to the right spot to watch the game. If life is worth living, then it should be taken seriously.

Soaking Up the Sun

Many came to The Beach in search of the sun and its warmth, and everyone has to accept the sun as a major factor of life here. The old man on the beach, whose skin is as golden brown as caramel and as wrinkled and tough-looking as leather, is a sun worshiper. His balding head and glowing nose are often protected, respectively, by a handkerchief hat and a napkin placed securely under the bridge of his sunglasses. His white-blond body hair and eyebrows reflect his discipline and dedication to life in the sun.

If the lady were younger she would be sporting a skimpy two-piece bathing suit, but at this time in her life the modest one-piece seems best. It's not that she's too old for beach life; it's more that she has accepted the fact that her body is, let's say, different than it was. She is aware of the taut, svelte body of the young Latin girl on the beach, and she likes to remember her time at that stage. But now she seems happy to walk along the shoreline, with her feet in the ebbing waves, and looks forward to admiring glances from the older boys on the beach.

There are those who wear their suntans as testimony. "I live on the beach," they cry out for all to hear and take notice. Some add schmaltz with gold chains and six-pointed stars or *chais*. And there are those who, unlike the lady in the one-piece suit, flaunt their fat, their bones, and their scars as if they were saying, "Look at me! I have lived and am still living!"

Living Together

After forty years of partnership it is easy to be together in the room. Everything they need is here, from the teakettle and the toaster, to the sofa bed and dinette, to the shelf on which it seems hundreds of family snapshots and wedding and graduation photographs are displayed.

In close proximity, within the room, they share every intimate detail of life. They know when they are kidding themselves or each other, and they know when they are serious. The room is called the apartment because it sounds better. The wail of the ambulance's siren has a personal kind of meaning and brings them closer together, even as it wanes into the distant night.

The candlesticks for *shabbos* which were once lit every Friday night are now displayed on a shelf across from the sofa bed. The Chanukah menorah around which the children stood for eight glorious nights in the "old house" waits patiently to be rediscovered. There are several *yahrzeit* candles in a box, to be lit on the anniversaries of deaths. The lighting of these candles brings back memories and signals the passing of time.

It's not that it's easier living together now than it used to be. But they are more grateful now, for having each other to trust and to love. And after all, they are living in paradise.

Living Alone

The apartment feels smaller even though there is only one now. The spirits of the past take up space in ways that defy the laws of physics. Life-filled pictures they once looked at together now look back with blank eyes.

The television set flickers, a replacement for life. They used to remind each other not to forget to light a *yahrzeit* candle for this one and that one—now who will remind the one who is left? Friday night brings services from Temple Israel on WTMI radio. They never really listened to the services when they were together; why listen now that they are apart? On the other hand, why not?

When they were together they almost never sat and looked through the box in which they kept the bills and receipts and important papers. Now this box seems more interesting. It contains the evidence of a life lived—a *ketubbah* (wedding contract) signed by the rabbi along with a marriage license signed by the clerk of the court from a northern city, photocopies of birth certificates, a deed to the cemetery plot that is waiting. This is an important box for two reasons: its contents define life as it has been and is being lived, and those same contents will be all that is left to define life in the end.

There really is no living alone. There is living with the past; with the problems and rewards of a longer life; with very special dogs or cats; and with death.

Dancing

Dancing alone is not how they dance on South Beach. On South Beach you either dance with a class or you dance with a partner.

Stretching and reaching and dancing in lines to music from a tape helps the memory—remember when you *could* stretch and bend? It makes you feel like you are part of a group. It makes you feel alive, even if life is accepted as a moderate muscle pain and the elixir of life is Ben-Gay.

Now dancing in couples is something else again. No matter if it is a square dance, a folk dance, or a fox-trot, it's nice to hold on to another and step lightly and gently together. Although men generally dance with women, women often dance with other women. It's all part of the social economy on The Beach.

The most fun is when the music is live and the small orchestra or ensemble can play requests and make the evening feel special. The dance is life's recital. For those who find dancing too difficult because of memories or physical maladies, these dances become concerts, and the music of an era past serves as a balm to ease the pain.

The men who offer up the music to those who listen and dance are proving to themselves and others that they are capable. They are in control of their fingers and their minds. They can remember how the music goes, and for the most part, while playing, they can forget the sad memories the music often calls to mind.

Along the walk east from Washington Avenue, the tropical beach fades and the huge old oaks, broad-leafed sea grapes, and the banyan trees with their sprawling canopies and dangling air roots grow in rows, denoting carefully drawn blocks. It's an urban street, but different from the others.

On Jefferson, Meridian, Euclid, and the other avenues there is a quiet calm—and also a feeling of loneliness and invisibility. Buildings are placed close together and the streets are lined with parked cars whose owners afraid to move them for fear of never being able to find another spot. In keeping with the unofficial requirement of Mediterranean design, local buildings often flaunt gardens and lanais adorned with sculptures and pastel ceramic tile murals.

There is life on the main streets and side streets of Miami Beach. On Washington Avenue there is life, death, and dying, all mixed up together.

From the porch of the Kenmore Hotel, the Avenue presents a long, narrow panorama of life at The Beach. Old City Hall, with its tall, stately tower, and the Main Post Office, with its polished stone and stained-glass crown, add majesty to this street. The Cameo Theatre is little more than a marquee and a shell of a movie house. To the south the Thrifty Supermarket is closed, no longer the scene of arguments over the last sale chicken or the last jar of "kosher for Passover" borscht. No community can live without remembering the past, and Washington Avenue serves in part as a community cemetery. But even in the face of death, life struggles on. The void left by the passing of "The Thrifty" is filled by Pantry Pride and the South Beach and Star supermarkets. On the northeast corner of Washington and 13th people buy produce. If ever there was an activity that demonstrated life in the South Beach fast lane, it's buying produce here. The sale of each and every melon is transacted with a certain savoir-faire which sets the beach shopper and the beach seller apart from their peers elsewhere. Here one contemplates the value of a ripe tomato with the same intensity that one devotes to the diversification of a financial portfolio. Here they call it *chutzpah*.

"Hey lady . . . don't squeeze the fruit until after you buy it," yells the greengrocer.

"I won't break it but I don't want it if it ain't right. [Pause and light squeeze.] Mister . . . seventy-nine a pound . . . what is this, gold?"

"Look, it's the frost . . . d'you want it or not?"

Knowing she has a good one in hand, and knowing that over her shoulder stands a competing customer, the shopper must decide. If she puts it down she'll never get it back, and if she takes it she'll know she got the best, not second best. "I'll take it," she says. "How about a taste of the honeydew . . . it don't look so good."

A sale and a taste is part of life on Washington Avenue. A careful listener enjoys the exchanges between these people, who are not angry or hostile but just doing business. There is a respect between the buyer and the seller. Each knows he or she needs the other to do business. After all, doing business is living.

Some go to the markets on Washington Avenue to shop while others go to forage for food. There are also those who simply steal, a way of winning at a time in life when victories are few. Not sure of who is who, the produce managers keep a watchful eye and there is a presumption of dishonesty in the air. Yet, on both sides of the shopping cart there is usually *rachmunos* (compassion) for those who must steal to live and disdain for those who just steal.

Kleptomania is often used here not so much as a description of a psychological disorder as an opportunity to rationalize and justify a socially unacceptable act. Both sides want dignity and respect. When an aging shoplifter is caught, who suffers? Do shopkeepers get pleasure from calling the police? Desperate times often force desperate actions. Sometimes life on Miami Beach is desperate.

From 1532 to 311 Washington Avenue, from the Jacob C. Cohen Community Synagogue to Beth Jacob Congregation, houses of spiritual healing abound. From Washington Avenue, the cross streets are branches that lead to still more places of worship, consolation, and study. Even apart from the *schuls*, the Jewish flavor of the street is unmistakable. On this street you can buy a kosher hot dog or corned beef sandwich, a *tallit* (prayer shawl) for a grandson's bar mitzvah, a set of candlesticks for a granddaughter's wedding, or even a copy of the Talmud for a scholar.

Window shopping on Washington Avenue is provocative. Who is wearing this new style and who wore that used dress now for sale? Since they don't make things like they used to, why not buy the old? Why not walk on—the dresses will still be here tomorrow.

Walking past the bakeries, fish stores, and restaurants provides the nose with a treat. Some smells are appetizing and jog the memory back to special events and occasions, while others are less pleasing but nonetheless familiar. Savoring the aromas affirms life, as does walking, talking, and watching the world go by on Washington Avenue.

Seasons

To the stranger there is but one season on Miami Beach. To those who live at The Beach the seasons change in perceptible ways. There is, of course, the tourist season which attracts the snowbirds from the north, who generally settle in the more plush nesting grounds north of South Beach. Flocks of these migratory birds blend together, creating a mixture of American, Canadian, and European species mingling with ease and bringing color to the local landscape.

On South Beach the season brings cooler weather. Sometimes it brings winter in a relatively vicious cold wave. Residents of South Beach turn to sweaters and blankets and other remnants of northern life for more than comfort—for survival.

The snowbirds often bring a new kind of life to South Beach. They swoop down on distant and not-so-distant relatives so as to "keep in touch." This instinctive ritual neutralizes guilt, while the prey of the snowbirds accept this attention, a *machia*—a gift from heaven—in a place where such gifts are not taken for granted.

Hurricane season is a time when Miami Beach confronts its physical vulnerability. Those who have not experienced the force of the winds and the pounding of the rain and waves listen carefully as they are told what dangers may lie ahead. There are shelters for protection and there are details one must not forget. As the two red-and-black ensigns are hoisted into the wind and the radio and TV call out the progress of the storm, people come together in quiet, anxious anticipation. After a storm passes, the power of nature and the value of life are reaffirmed.

The seasons also revolve around the holidays. In the fall it's the New Year. Rosh Hashanah, Yom Kippur, and Sukkoth are observed—by many with a glance, by others with special foods, fasts, and ceremonies. In the spring there is always Pesach (Passover), the festival of freedom. It seems that this ancient festival is the most widely celebrated of all the holidays. Virtually everyone has at least some matzoh as a means of participation and connection—and the community makes sure that all who want it have matzoh. Pesach calls out to everyone in Miami Beach: "Live as a free person among others who are free." It is a season of emancipation, a season of renewal.

Faces

Look through the eyes of a person who has lived a long time, and see life from a different perspective. Look at the way people hold up their heads and know if they've been humbled and beaten or if they're strong and purposeful. Look directly into their faces and know something about their journeys.

There are faces full of appreciation and gratitude when a free hot meal is delivered to their apartment. They understand that this is an act of community, an act to strengthen and to sustain rather than to humiliate. There are faces that smile at the bus drivers, counselors, and therapists provided by the various Jewish community agencies. There are faces filled with joy at being cared for, at being a person whose needs seem to matter.

On the other hand, there are faces who reject the attention they receive, because they don't want charity—it's one thing to give and a very different thing to receive. Some of these faces are angry and some are desperate. These faces speak of dreams lost and hopes dashed.

There also are blank, flat faces which do not even stare. These faces simply exist. Nothing is divulged about life except that it has been endured. No help is sought, though help is generally offered. These faces may find their way to Douglas Gardens or other less prestigious nursing homes. Here, perhaps, they will find peace.

But mostly the faces on the Beach are lit by shining eyes that give testimony to life. Each wrinkle and each scar has been earned, and the smiles are genuine even if the teeth are not.

If you ever get to Miami Beach, don't forget to look squarely into each face. You'll usually get a smile back and you might be asked if you're Jewish.

Newcomers

Miami Beach is dynamic. The beaches are constantly remodeled by natural forces. So it is with the people. Vacancies and voids are filled naturally. Death frees special chairs in the lobbies of residential hotels, allowing others to move up in station. Apartments are vacated by those who die and by those who move, and rents go up and down.

Today there are cigar-smoking Cubans in white *guayabera* shirts playing dominoes in the park. Many share an eastern European heritage with their neighbors.

They communicate in neither English nor Spanish . . . they speak to each other in Yiddish. These newcomers have established their *schuls* and are settled into life on South Beach.

Moving into old restored hotels and apartments in the South Beach Preservation District is a new community of young and often gay newcomers. Their vibrant presence is felt and seen on Española Way and along Ocean Drive. A stylish Art Deco attitude and a spirit of living life fully permeate this neighborhood, and Miami Beach is richer for it.

There are Jews from Russia in South Beach, many more Russian than Jewish, and there are Asians and Haitians as well. On occasion Canadians find their way down from the north (North Miami and parts of Broward County, that is). Virtually everybody finds a place on The Beach. If you live long enough you realize that there is more to gain through coexistence than there is through the closing of a mind, the blocking out of an experience, or the rejecting of another.

The newcomers lack a history of life on The Beach. No matter. They are part of life there now and they'll make their history.

Reflections

Each week some time is found to reflect back upon a lifetime. This time is sometimes found in a dream, sometimes while looking through a box of memories. Here is what life comes down to: passbooks and checkbooks, cards—membership, insurance, and Social Security—and papers (once very official and important and now not so important, except for the will). Photographs are important and so is the vault key. Every child knows about the vault key, although few know what the vault presently contains. No doubt about it, the deed for the cemetery plot will be found in the vault.

Looking back, life really was what we made it. Friends count more than money, and social status is now fixed. Trust is valued more than interest, as the dividends of trust are more precious in these final days.

In the mirror I see how I am and I know if I can face myself. Today I am the only one whose judgment counts.

Sitting in a webbed-back aluminum chair securely resting on the tiles of the porch, I look out and remember the shadows of the night. The reflections of a frightening time are brought home to me as I recall the pictures from the Holocaust and the piles of eyeglasses, suitcases, and shoes stacked up in the camps.

As I walk the streets I see the clothing in the secondhand stores and thrift shops. Tonight I ask myself questions about the quality of life. Are these the questions of an old Jew or are these questions asked by everyone as they turn to look back?

I see the young walking by. They are different from us when we were young, and yet they are the same. I was different from those who came ahead of me and I was angered by their lack of respect for me. I don't think I pushed back very hard and I wish that I had. Should I now respect these new young ones? Should I envy them? I do!

On the porch I sit and look out and I don't talk very much anymore. It looks as though I am contemplating important issues, but I am really waiting to go to bed. A better peace may await me in the night.

It is impossible to look too far ahead, and a distinct possibility that I will look so far back as to lose my hold on reality. The fear of slipping away from reality is real because it is difficult to resist the temptation to let go and be done with it.

Molokh ha-Mavet, the Angel of Death, is no stranger to Miami Beach. He waits behind every palm tree on the beach and every club chair in each and every lobby. His presence is known to all and he is respected—a prominent citizen of Miami Beach. However, there is one thing that sets this citizen apart from all others: he knows no difference between South Beach and the Sea Coast Towers. He treats guests in the Hotel Chelsea exactly the same as he treats guests at the Fontainebleau Hilton.

In every other way, Molokh ha-Mavet is just another citizen of The Beach. Most people don't know who he is when he shows up, and when he leaves there is so much to do that there is no time to think about him.

Miami Beach is a place where people die. But it is much more than that. As hard as it is to remember, Miami Beach is a place where people come to live.

Miami Beach. *L'Chaim!* To life!

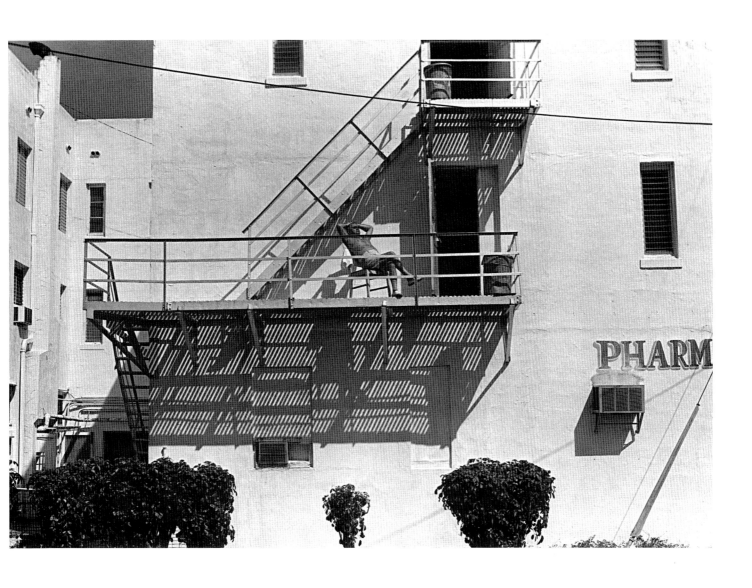

Sunbather, South Beach.

Joe's Stone Crabs. While other buildings in the area were being condemned, this restaurant was given landmark status. I was led to believe that the owner had a relative involved in local politics.

A rabbi's house in South Beach.

Picking up people for the Free Lunch Program in South Beach.

South Beach Community Center.

Mrs. Shoenfeld in her kitchen.

Mrs. Shoenfeld's bureau.

Mrs. Sharf with the medallion that her son had just sent her from Caesar's Palace in Las Vegas.

This man was called "The Chairman." At the end of the day, when he awoke from his nap, I learned how he had earned this title: he carefully arranged the chairs in rows.

Taking a break from poolside bingo at the Shellborne Hotel.

Shoeshine in Bal Harbour.

Patron of Tony's Barber Shop, getting a shave and a manicure.

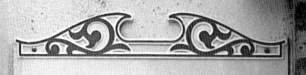

PERRY
CHESTER
SHOE SALONS

The Better Look
Skin Clinic, Inc.

BEFORE   **AFTER**

TONY
& NINA
ALTERATIONS

Friday afternoon, getting ready for *shabbat*.

View from the Steinsapiers' patio at the Seacoast Towers.

View from the Korns' patio, South Beach.

Clothing store, Washington Avenue.

Afternoon prayers at a rooming house.

Taking a nap under *The Daily Forward.*

"I should have gone to Arizona."

Label, reminiscing about coming to America. He told his mother that he had received a letter from his brother asking that he join him in America. His lie succeeded and his mother let him go.

Fishing pier, South Beach. I never saw anybody catch anything, but everyone was always smiling.

Rifkala at the Shellborne Hotel.

Eugene Klein. "When I had a stroke it was the thought that I would be back playing with the orchestra that gave me the will to live."

Joe Garelik, 90, mandolin player; Harry Rose, 92, cellist; and Eugene Klein, 90, violinist—on the evening they were honored by the Senior Citizens Orchestra.

Saturday night.

Lunchtime, Rebecca Towers. Thanks to the hard work of many people, especially a community worker named Max Serchuck, a low-income housing project was erected for the residents of South Beach. Rebecca Towers was one of the sites for the Meals On Wheels program. The local paper reported that the "kosher" meals they were serving were probably not kosher at all.

One of the most impressive aspects of the lunch program was the sense of family that evolved. If you did not show up for a meal, the others would always check to see if you were in need.

Shoplifting is a problem in Miami Beach. Besides the many warning signs and posters, a security guard is posted at the door. I had been told by many residents that often they would take something off the shelf, start heading for the cashier, meet up with a friend, and forget to pay. I observed several instances when security people, rather than tactfully saying, "Have you paid for this item?", grabbed seniors by the arm and marched them across the store to call the police. The punishment for those caught stealing was the ultimate humiliation; your name and crime were published in the following day's newspaper.

The Thrifty Market, Washington Avenue.

Abe Marcus, community activist in South Beach.

Mr. and Mrs. Korn of South Beach.

I noticed there were many people sitting at the bus stops, yet the buses were generally empty. I realized that not all the people were waiting for the bus; the activity there was a way of keeping busy and feeling involved.

Mr. Horowitz, outside the Habana Hotel. Mr. Horowitz kept his money in his mattress, hiding it from his children, so that when he died his friends would send the money to Israel.

Wolfie's Restaurant, a favorite.

Tony's Barber Shop.

Mr. and Mrs. Wasserman. The same people sit together every day. Day after day, year after year, that's their seat, that's their spot. Sometimes they don't even talk to each other. But if one day you are not there, someone is sure to check up on you. This is the strength of a concentrated retirement community.

The Berkeley Shores.

Shuffleboard at Flamingo Park. While watching this game I had the good fortune of sitting next to an old pro who informed me of all the rules and strategies. He told me, "These people play all year round, every day. They can't see or hear but they are pretty tolerant of each other." There were occasional arguments, but even these were good-natured. Hanging around one of these games, you hear a lot of talk about "the kitchen," which is the penalty section of the shuffleboard court.

Cuban domino players. While walking on Meridian Avenue, I stopped to watch this game. The men switched from Spanish to English as a way of letting me know I was welcome.

By the pool at the Americana Hotel.

This gentleman spent a lot of time sitting by the women's bathroom, making conversation with the women as they went in and out.

Joe Stern.

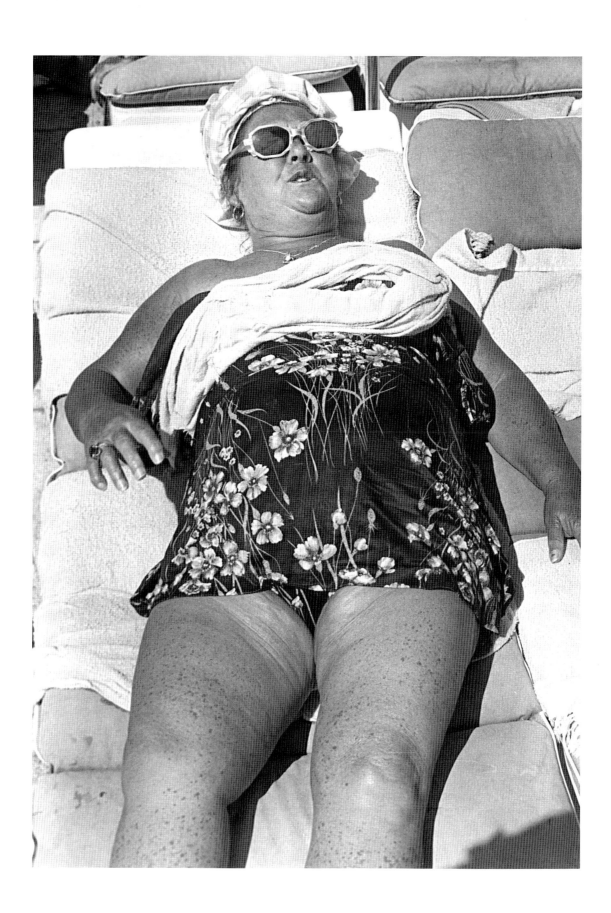

Washington Avenue. Medical needs were advertised and promoted in a very exciting manner. Pharmacies have assemblages of weight, blood pressure, and heart rate machines that could easily be mistaken for a pinball game in a penny arcade.

Shoe repair shop, Washington Avenue.

Washington Avenue. This woman's only view to the street is through this hallway.